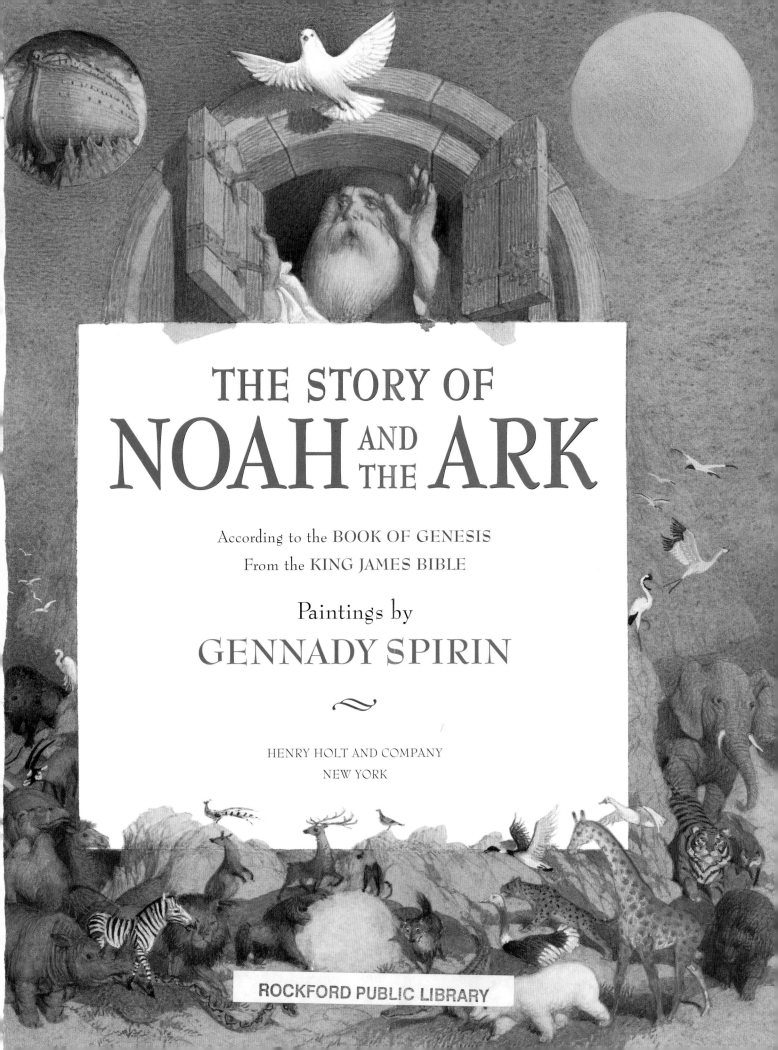

# THE STORY OF
# NOAH AND THE ARK

According to the BOOK OF GENESIS
From the KING JAMES BIBLE

## Paintings by
# GENNADY SPIRIN

HENRY HOLT AND COMPANY
NEW YORK

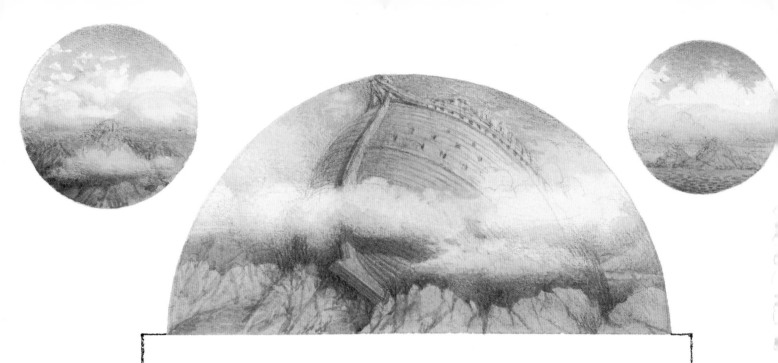

Henry Holt and Company, LLC
*Publishers since 1866*
115 West 18th Street
New York, New York 10011
www.henryholt.com

Henry Holt is a registered
trademark of Henry Holt and Company, LLC
Illustrations copyright © 2004 by Gennady Spirin
Distributed in Canada by H. B. Fenn and Company Ltd.

Library of Congress Cataloging-in-Publication Data
Bible. O.T. Genesis VI–IX. English. Authorized. Selections. 2004.
The story of Noah and the ark: according to the book of Genesis:
from the King James Bible / paintings by Gennady Spirin.
p.   cm.
Summary: Illustrations accompany the biblical text telling how Noah obeyed God's command
to build an ark in order to survive the great flood.
[1. Noah (biblical figure). 2. Noah's ark. 3. Bible stories—O.T.]   I. Spirin, Gennady, ill.   II. Title.
BS1233 2004   222'.1109505—dc22   2003013020

ISBN 0-8050-6181-9 / First Edition—2004 / Designed by Patrick Collins
The artist used tempera, watercolor, and pencil on watercolor paper to create the illustrations for this book.
Manufactured in China
1  3  5  7  9  10  8  6  4  2

*To the memory of Mikhail Shvartsman*

∾

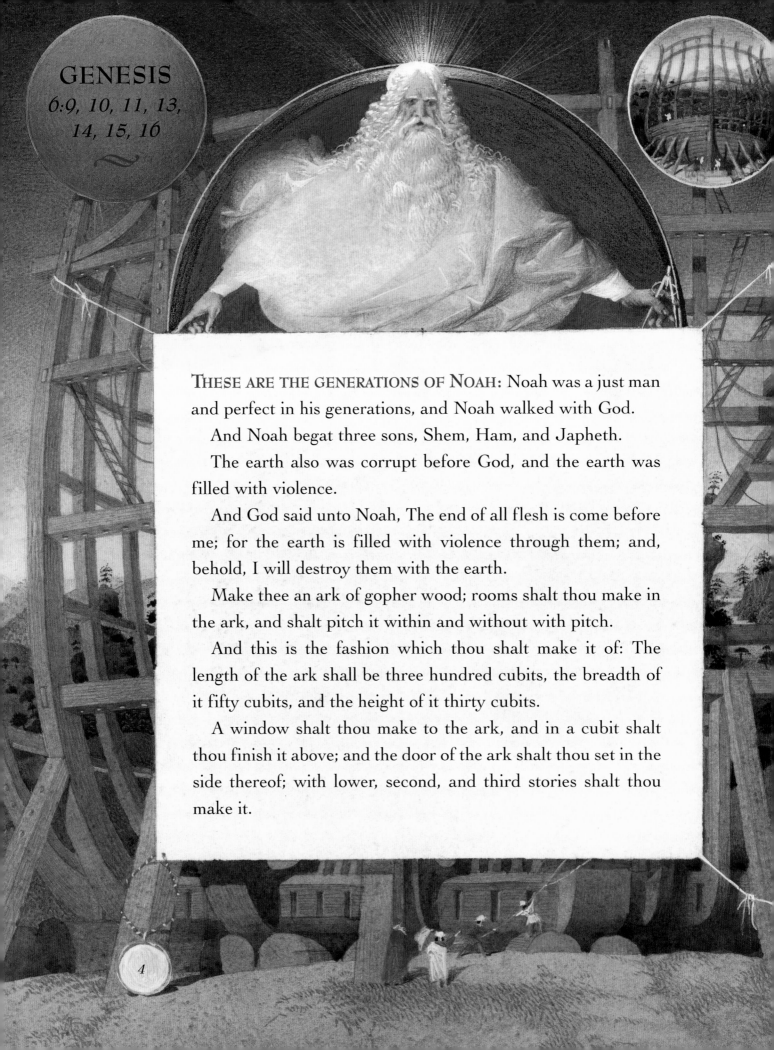

THESE ARE THE GENERATIONS OF NOAH: Noah was a just man and perfect in his generations, and Noah walked with God.

And Noah begat three sons, Shem, Ham, and Japheth.

The earth also was corrupt before God, and the earth was filled with violence.

And God said unto Noah, The end of all flesh is come before me; for the earth is filled with violence through them; and, behold, I will destroy them with the earth.

Make thee an ark of gopher wood; rooms shalt thou make in the ark, and shalt pitch it within and without with pitch.

And this is the fashion which thou shalt make it of: The length of the ark shall be three hundred cubits, the breadth of it fifty cubits, and the height of it thirty cubits.

A window shalt thou make to the ark, and in a cubit shalt thou finish it above; and the door of the ark shalt thou set in the side thereof; with lower, second, and third stories shalt thou make it.

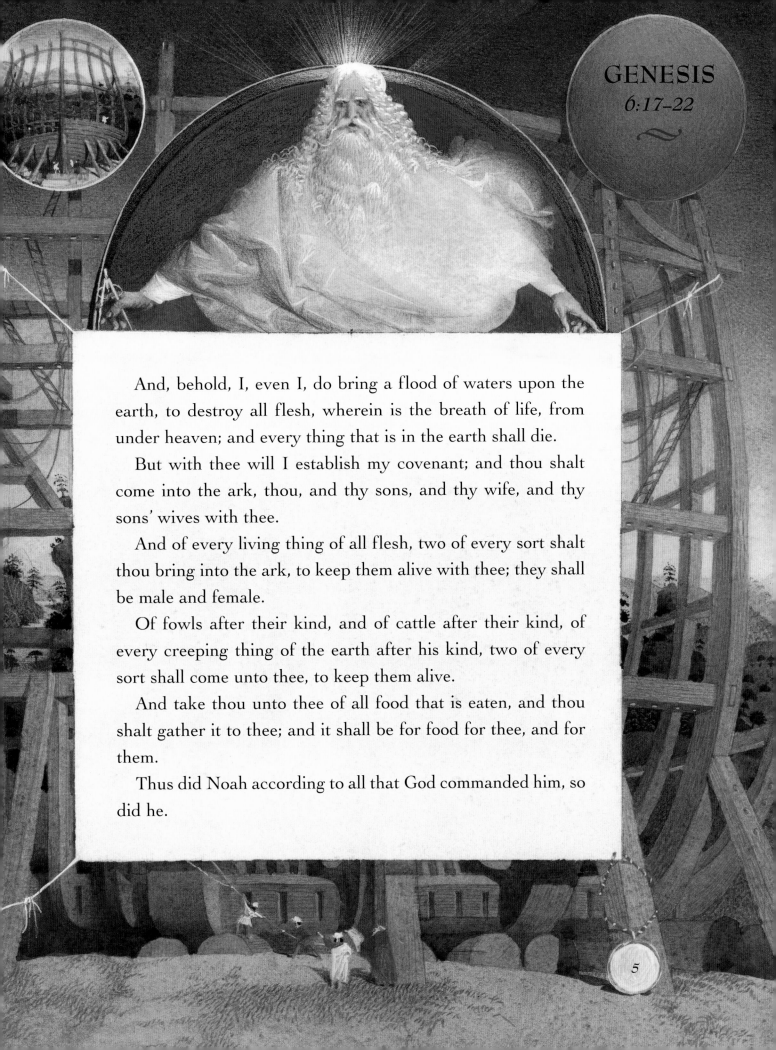

And, behold, I, even I, do bring a flood of waters upon the earth, to destroy all flesh, wherein is the breath of life, from under heaven; and every thing that is in the earth shall die.

But with thee will I establish my covenant; and thou shalt come into the ark, thou, and thy sons, and thy wife, and thy sons' wives with thee.

And of every living thing of all flesh, two of every sort shalt thou bring into the ark, to keep them alive with thee; they shall be male and female.

Of fowls after their kind, and of cattle after their kind, of every creeping thing of the earth after his kind, two of every sort shall come unto thee, to keep them alive.

And take thou unto thee of all food that is eaten, and thou shalt gather it to thee; and it shall be for food for thee, and for them.

Thus did Noah according to all that God commanded him, so did he.

And the LORD said unto Noah, Come thou and all thy house into the ark; for thee have I seen righteous before me in this generation.

And Noah went in, and his sons, and his wife, and his sons' wives with him, into the ark, because of the waters of the flood.

And it came to pass after seven days, that the waters of the flood were upon the earth.

And the rain was upon the earth forty days and forty nights.

And the waters prevailed, and were increased greatly upon the earth; and the ark went upon the face of the waters.

14

And the waters prevailed exceedingly upon the earth; and all the high hills, that were under the whole heaven, were covered.

And every living substance was destroyed which was upon the face of the ground, both man, and cattle, and the creeping things, and the fowl of the heaven; and they were destroyed from the earth: and Noah only remained alive, and they that were with him in the ark.

And the waters prevailed upon the earth an hundred and fifty days.

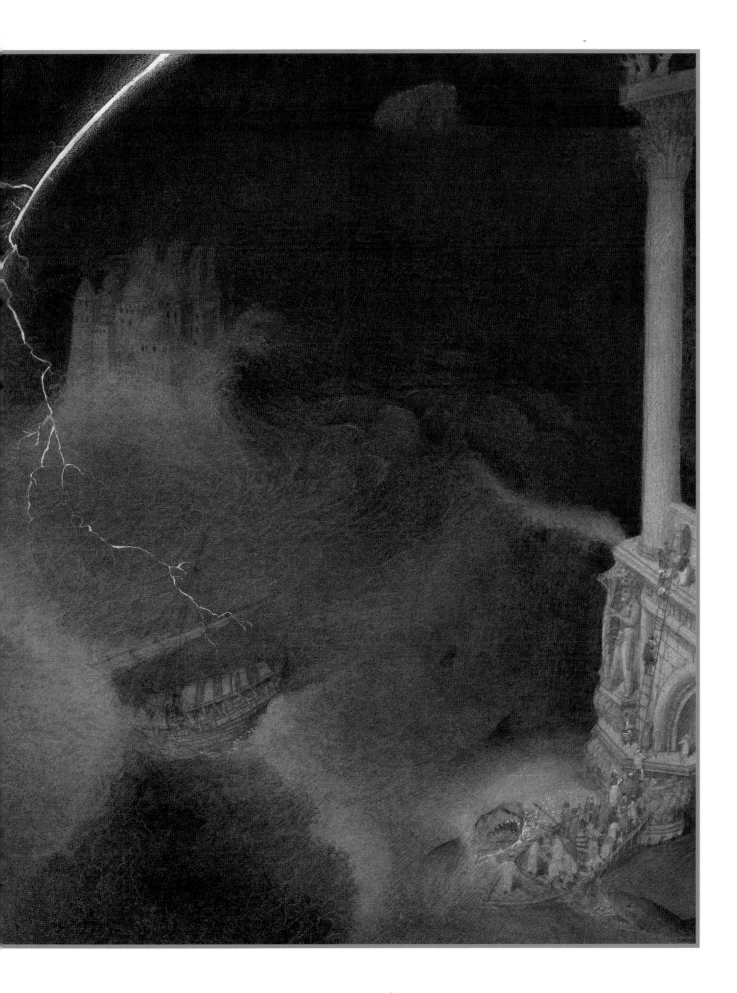

And God remembered Noah, and every living thing, and all the cattle that was with him in the ark: and God made a wind to pass over the earth, and the waters assuaged;

The fountains also of the deep and the windows of heaven were stopped, and the rain from heaven was restrained;

And the waters returned from off the earth continually: and after the end of the hundred and fifty days the waters were abated.

And the ark rested in the seventh month, on the seventeenth day of the month, upon the mountains of Ararat.

And the waters decreased continually until the tenth month: in the tenth month, on the first day of the month, were the tops of the mountains seen.

And it came to pass at the end of forty days, that Noah opened the window of the ark which he had made:

And he sent forth a raven, which went forth to and fro, until the waters were dried up from off the earth.

Also he sent forth a dove from him, to see if the waters were abated from off the face of the ground;

But the dove found no rest for the sole of her foot, and she returned unto him into the ark, for the waters were on the face of the whole earth: then he put forth his hand, and took her, and pulled her in unto him into the ark.

And he stayed yet other seven days; and again he sent forth the dove out of the ark;

And the dove came in to him in the evening; and, lo, in her mouth was an olive leaf pluckt off: so Noah knew that the waters were abated from off the earth.

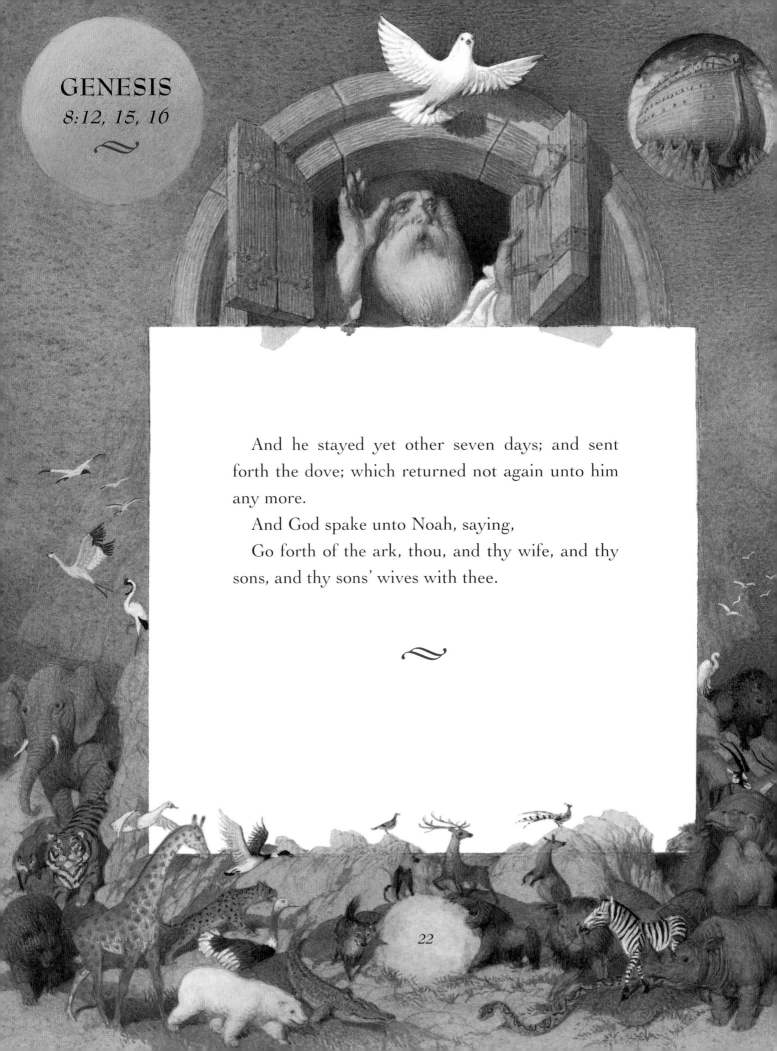

And he stayed yet other seven days; and sent forth the dove; which returned not again unto him any more.

And God spake unto Noah, saying,

Go forth of the ark, thou, and thy wife, and thy sons, and thy sons' wives with thee.

Bring forth with thee every living thing that is with thee, of all flesh, both of fowl, and of cattle, and of every creeping thing that creepeth upon the earth; that they may breed abundantly in the earth, and be fruitful, and multiply upon the earth.

And Noah went forth, and his sons, and his wife, and his sons' wives with him:

Every beast, every creeping thing, and every fowl, and whatsoever creepeth upon the earth, after their kinds, went forth out of the ark.

And God blessed Noah and his sons, and said unto them, Be fruitful, and multiply, and replenish the earth.

And the fear of you and the dread of you shall be upon every beast of the earth, and upon every fowl of the air, upon all that moveth upon the earth, and upon all the fishes of the sea; into your hand are they delivered.

Every moving thing that liveth shall be meat for you; even as the green herb have I given you all things.

And I will establish my covenant with you; neither shall all flesh be cut off any more by the waters of a flood; neither shall there any more be a flood to destroy the earth.

And God said, This is the token of the covenant which I make between me and you and every living creature that is with you, for perpetual generations:

I do set my bow in the cloud, and it shall be for a token of a covenant between me and the earth.

## ABOUT THE ILLUSTRATOR

Gennady Spirin was born on Christmas Day in 1948 in a small city near Moscow, in Russia. He is a graduate of the Stroganov Academy of Fine Arts in Moscow and has received many awards for his work both nationally and internationally.

Mr. Spirin lives in Princeton, New Jersey, with his wife and three sons.

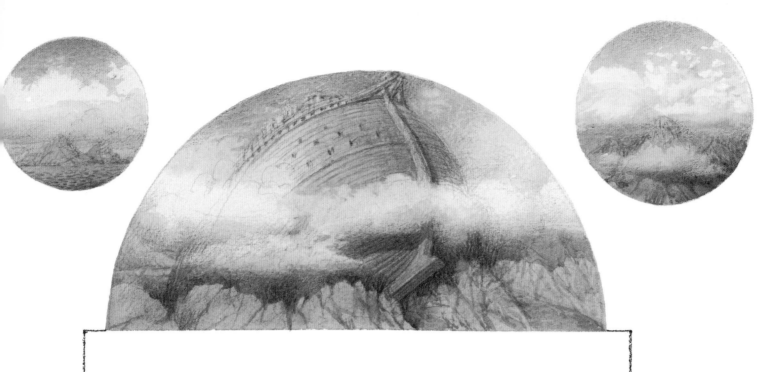

## ABOUT THE STORY

Accounts of a great flood have been found in the records of ancient civilizations like those on tablets from Mesopotamia. This story is also a part of the folklore of peoples from various parts of the globe, such as Australia, the Americas, and New Guinea.

Today archaeologists, geologists, and other enthusiasts continue to look for evidence of Noah's ark and of a great flood.